NICHOLA PALMER
SOUPS AND STARTERS

KU-168-930

Produced by New Leaf Productions, Ashford, Kent

Photography by Mick Duff
Design by Jim Wire
Typeset by System Graphics Ltd., Folkestone
Series Editor: James M. Gibson

First published in 1987 by
Hamlyn Publishing
Bridge House, 69 London Road
Twickenham, Middlesex, England

Copyright © The Hamlyn Publishing Group Limited 1987

ISBN 0 600 327000

Printed in Hong Kong

All rights reserved. No part of this publication may be reproduced, stored in a retrieval system, or transmitted in any form or by any means, electronic, mechanical, photocopying, recording or otherwise, without the permission of the Hamlyn Publishing Group Limited.

We would like to thank: Reject China Shops (branches in London, Windsor, Bath, Chester, York, Canterbury, Stratford-upon-Avon and Oxford) and NASONS of Canterbury for the loan of the china used in photography; Susie Theodoran for her help with recipe testing; Tricia Payne for her help with photography; and Glyn Palmer for all his support and encouragement.

CONTENTS

INTRODUCTION

The main course may seem like the most important part of a meal, but the starter, which whets the appetite for the main course, is just as important, if not more so, and should be treated accordingly.

Starters and soups should be tasty and served in small portions to prevent dulling the appetite. It is a great temptation to get stuck into a large plate of pasta or bowl of soup with crusty bread on a cold winter's evening to quell the hunger pangs, but this will only ruin the rest of the meal. If serving pasta, for example, serve a small quantity and plan the rest of the meal accordingly: follow with a light fish or chicken dish, not steak and kidney pie.

When planning a meal, think in terms of a variety of colours, shapes, flavours and textures. Also think of yourself, the cook; dinner will be no fun if every course needs last minute attention. Soups and cold starters are probably the most popular way to start a meal because they are 'well-behaved' and not likely to cause last minute panics. But, with a little planning a hot starter can be no trouble and makes an impressive start to a meal.

Of course, it goes without saying that most of the soups and starters in this book can also be served as snacks or light meals. Just add some crusty bread or soda bread and salad if applicable. Allow larger portions than served for a starter; a recipe which serves six as a starter will probably serve four as a snack.

MAKING STOCK

It is hard to go wrong with a soup, but a good home-made stock greatly improves the finished flavour of the soup. An appropriate flavoured stock cube can be used if necessary instead of making your own stock, but use it in a dilute form, 1 cube per 600 ml/1 pint of water. Stock cubes also tend to be salty, so take this into account when adding extra salt.

VEGETABLE STOCK
Makes 1.75 litres/3 pints

2 carrots, peeled and chopped
1 onion, chopped
1 leek, washed and chopped
1 celery stick, chopped
1.75 litres/3 pints water
6 black peppercorns
1 bay leaf
1 sprig parsley

Place all the ingredients in a large saucepan and slowly bring to the boil, removing any scum as it rises to the surface. Cover and simmer for 45 minutes. Strain through a cloth-lined sieve and cool.

Variations on vegetable stock
Beef Stock—Add 450 g/1 lb chopped shin of beef or marrow bones to the pan with the vegetables. Cover and simmer for 3 hours. Check water level occasionally and top up if necessary. Strain through a cloth-lined sieve. When the stock is cool, skim off the fat.
Ham Stock—Add 450 g/1 lb chopped knuckle or shank bone to the pan with the vegetables. Cover and simmer for 3 hours. Check water level occasionally and top up if necessary. Strain through a cloth-lined sieve. When the stock is cool, skim off the fat.
Chicken Stock—Add 1 chicken carcass broken into pieces to the pan with the vegetables. Cook for 1 hour. Strain through a cloth-lined sieve. When the stock is cool, skim off the fat.
Fish Stock—Add 350 g/12 oz fish trimmings (bones, heads and tails) to the pan with the vegetables. Cook for 30 minutes. Strain through a cloth-lined sieve.

Making stock in the pressure cooker
Bring the stock to the boil, cover and bring to 15 lb pressure. Cook for one-third of the times given above.

Making stock in the microwave
Chicken, fish and vegetable stocks are successful in the microwave. Place 900 ml/1½ pints water in a large microwave-proof bowl with the remaining ingredients. Cover with cling film and pierce two holes in the top. Cook on full power for 20 minutes for vegetable and fish stocks, 30 minutes for chicken stock. Strain and add remaining water.

Freezing stock
All stock freezes well except fish stock, which should be made fresh as required. Freeze the cooled, strained and skimmed stocks in plastic boxes. Use within six months. For smaller quantities freeze the stock in ice cube trays (noting how much they hold). When the stock is frozen, transfer the cubes to a plastic bag. The frozen cubes can then be stirred into soups or sauces as required.

GARNISHES

Garnishing a soup will not only enhance its appearance, but will also add flavour and texture. Even a sprinkling of chopped chives or parsley can do wonders for a soup which looks dull and lifeless. Here are a selection of simple garnishes.

Double Cream or Thick Yogurt—spoon a swirl of cream or natural yogurt on the soup just before serving. To 'feather' the swirl, run a cocktail stick backwards and forwards through the cream.

Puff Pastry Shapes—Roll out puff pastry trimmings and cut into diamonds or fancy shapes with small cutters. Brush with egg, sprinkle with poppy seeds or sesame seeds, if liked, and bake in a preheated hot oven (220°C, 425°F, gas 7) for 5-10 minutes until golden.

Vegetable Sticks—cut carrot, peppers, courgettes or leeks into thin matchstick-sized strips. Cook in boiling salted water for 2 minutes. Drain.

Bacon Rolls—stretch bacon rashers with the back of a knife, roll up and grill until crisp.
Bacon Snippets—Grill bacon rashers until crisp. Cool and chop into small pieces.

Tomato Concassé—Dip ripe tomatoes in hot water for 30 seconds, peel off the skin, remove the seeds and chop the flesh.

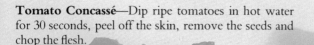

Fried Croutons—Cut thick slices of bread into cubes. Fry in hot oil until golden, then drain. For variety flavour with garlic (fry with 1 clove garlic in the oil, or sprinkle with garlic salt), sprinkle with Parmesan cheese or onion salt, or add curry powder to the oil.
Toasted Croutons—Toast bread on both sides and cut into cubes. To flavour, toast one side, spread untoasted side with garlic butter, or peanut butter or sprinkle with cheese and grill, then cut into cubes.

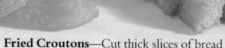

Carrot Flowers—peel and thinly slice a large carrot and cut out flowers with a fluted cutter. Cook in boiling salted water for 2 minutes. Drain.

Spinach Shreds—trim the stalks off fresh spinach leaves. Roll up the leaves and slice thinly.

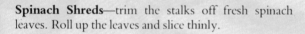

Fried Onion Rings.

Chopped Fresh Herbs
—parsley, chives, coriander or basil.

ACCOMPANIMENTS

Any soup tastes better when accompanied by crusty bread, croutons, or crackers. To avoid competing flavours, serve a bland accompaniment, like melba toast or soda bread, with a heavily flavoured soup and a more distinctive accompaniment, like garlic bread, with a milder soup.

Dumplings—For 12 dumplings (to serve 6) mix together 100 g/4 oz self-raising flour, 50 g/2 oz shredded suet, salt and pepper, and 150 ml/¼ pint water, to make an elastic dough. Shape into small balls and add to the hot soup. Cover and simmer for 15 minutes. Flavour with 2 tablespoons chopped parsley or 2 teaspoons caraway seeds or 2 teaspoons mustard powder or 1 tablespoon grated onion.

Cheese Croutes—Toast and butter one slice of French bread per person. Grate just over 15 g/½ oz Gruyere cheese per person and pile onto the toast. Grill to melt the cheese. Place one in each bowl of soup.

Garlic Bread—Beat together 100 g/4 oz softened butter, 1-2 crushed cloves of garlic, 2 tablespoons chopped parsley, salt and freshly ground black pepper. Slice a French stick or a long roll, taking care not to cut right through. Spread the garlic butter over both sides of each slice. Wrap the slices in foil and cook in a preheated hot oven (220°C, 425°F, gas 7) 20 minutes for a French stick, 10 minutes for rolls. Open up the foil for the last few minutes to give a crisp crust. For herb bread, omit the garlic and add 2 teaspoons mixed dried herbs.

Melba Toast—Toast thin slices of bread on both sides. Cut off crusts and slice bread through the middle. Cut in half diagonally and grill untoasted side. The toast will curl, but watch to prevent it from burning.

Soda Bread—Sift together 225 g/8 oz plain flour, a pinch of salt, 1 teaspoon bicarbonate of soda and ½ teaspoon cream of tartar. Rub in 50 g/2 oz butter. Then stir in 1 egg, beaten with 75 ml/3 fl oz milk to make a smooth dough. Shape into a large round, place on a greased baking tray and cut into 8 equal wedges. Bake in a preheated moderately hot oven (200°C, 400°F, gas 6) for 20-25 minutes until well risen and golden. Serve warm. For variety use wholemeal flour or half white flour, half wholemeal flour.

Cheese and Carrot Soda Bread—Stir 100 g/4 oz grated mature cheese and 100 g/4 oz grated carrot into the rubbed in soda bread mixture. Sprinkle with grated cheese and cayenne pepper before baking.

Tomato Herb Soda Bread—Add 50 g/2 oz grated onion, 1 teaspoon mixed dried herbs and 2 tablespoons chopped fresh parsley to the rubbed in soda bread mixture. Add 2 tablespoons tomato purée to the egg and milk. Sprinkle with sesame seeds before baking.

THIN SOUPS

CLASSIC CONSOMMÉ

Serves 6

A well flavoured home-made stock is essential for this soup. The stock and all utensils must be free from grease to ensure a crystal clear result. The egg white acts as a filter to make the soup sparkle.

1.15 litres/2 pints cold beef stock (see page 4)
1 carrot, peeled and quartered
1 small onion, quartered
bouquet garni
1 egg white
salt
2 teaspoons dry sherry

Remove any fat from the surface of the stock and pour the stock into a large saucepan. Add the carrot, onion and bouquet garni. Add the egg white and heat gently, whisking continuously until a thick froth starts to form. Stop whisking and bring to the boil. Reduce the heat, cover and simmer gently for 1 hour. Strain the soup through a scalded jelly bag or double thickness of muslin into a bowl. Return the consommé to a clean pan and reheat. Add salt to taste and stir in the sherry.

A garnish can be added at this stage just before serving. The garnish should be cooked and rinsed before adding it to the consommé to prevent if from going cloudy. The consommé then takes its name from the garnish used.

CONSOMMÉ JULIENNE

Cut vegetables, such as carrot, celery, and parsnip, into thin matchstick-sized pieces. Cook in boiling salted water until just tender, rinse and add to Classic Consommé just before serving.

CONSOMMÉ a L'ITALIENNE

Cook some tiny soup pasta, such as letters, stars, or wheels, in boiling salted water until tender. Allow 25g/1 oz per 500 ml/1 pint Classic Consommé. Rinse and add to Classic Consommé just before serving.

CONSOMMÉ a la JARDINIÈRE

Prepare a mixture of vegetables, such as carrots sliced and cut into shapes with an aspic cutter, tiny florets of cauliflower, sliced tiny button mushrooms, and some shredded lettuce leaves. Cook in boiling salted water until just tender. Drain and rinse. Add to the Classic Consommé just before serving.

CONSOMMÉ PRINCESSE

Add cooked, drained and rinsed or canned asparagus tips to the Classic Consommé just before serving. Allow about three asparagus tips per serving.

FRENCH ONION SOUP
Serves 6

Use Spanish onions, if available, to make this soup.

25 g/1 oz butter
450 g/1 lb onions, peeled and sliced
1.15 litres/2 pints beef stock (see page 4)
salt and freshly ground black pepper
1 tablespoon cornflour
4 tablespoons cold water
6 Cheese Croutes (see page 8)

Melt the butter in a large saucepan. Add the onions, stir well to coat in butter, cover and cook over a gentle heat for about 15 minutes to soften. Uncover, increase the heat and lightly brown the onions. Stir in the stock, salt and pepper and bring to the boil. Reduce the heat and simmer for about 20 minutes. Mix the cornflour with the water to form a smooth paste. Stir into the soup, bring to the boil, stirring, until thickened. Simmer for 2 minutes and taste for seasoning. Place a Cheese Croute in each soup bowl and ladle the soup over the top. Serve immediately.

CRAB AND SWEET CORN SOUP
Serves 4 to 6

1.15 litres/2 pints chicken stock (see page 4)
198-g/7-oz can sweet corn kernels, drained
2 spring onions, chopped
2 tablespoons cornflour
1 tablespoon dry sherry
salt and freshly ground black pepper
170-g/6-oz can crabmeat
1 large carrot, cut into flowers and cooked (see page 7)

Heat the stock, sweet corn and spring onions together in a saucepan. Bring to the boil, reduce the heat and simmer for 5 minutes. Mix the cornflour with the sherry to form a smooth paste and pour into the soup, stirring. Bring to the boil, stirring, and simmer for 2 minutes. Whisk in the crabmeat, add the carrot flowers and season to taste. Serve hot.

THICK SOUPS

TUSCAN BEAN SOUP
Serves 6

If time is short, use a 425-g/15-oz can of haricot beans and a 225-g/8-oz can of red kidney beans; this eliminates the overnight soaking and reduces cooking time to about 30 minutes.

225 g/8 oz dried haricot beans
100 g/4 oz dried red kidney beans
3 tablespoons olive oil
1 small onion, chopped
1 small carrot, peeled and chopped
50 g/2 oz rindless unsmoked bacon, finely
   chopped
2 cloves garlic, finely chopped
1.15 litres/2 pints beef stock (see page 4)
salt and freshly ground black pepper
2 large beefsteak tomatoes
100 g/4 oz cheese, grated

Soak the beans in cold water overnight. Bring to the boil and boil hard for 3 minutes, reduce heat and simmer for a further 10 minutes. Drain.

Heat the oil in a large pan and cook the onion, carrot and bacon until the onion is just soft but not brown. Add the garlic, beans and stock. Bring to the boil, cover and simmer for about 1 hour until the beans are soft. Blend half the soup in a food processor or liquidiser until smooth and return to the pan with the remaining soup. Cut a cross in the base of each tomato and dip into boiling water for 30 seconds. Peel off the skin, cut into quarters, remove the seeds and chop the flesh. Add the tomatoes to the soup with seasoning to taste. Simmer for about 15 minutes. Serve the soup sprinkled with cheese accompanied by garlic bread (see page 8).

PEPPER POT SOUP
Serves 6

In Jamaica where this soup originates, pigs' tails are included in the list of ingredients. This is my adaptation of the recipe using ingredients available in this country. To make coconut milk, dissolve 40 g/1½ oz creamed coconut in 100 ml/4 fl oz hot water.

25 g/1 oz butter
1 onion, chopped
1 clove garlic, crushed
450 g/1 lb spinach, washed
6 okra, thinly sliced
2 green chillies, halved
1 sprig thyme
1.15 litres/2 pints beef stock (see page 4)
salt and freshly ground black pepper
198-g/7-oz can peeled, cooked shrimps or
    prawns
150 ml/¼ pint coconut milk

Heat the butter in a large saucepan, add the onion, garlic, spinach, okra, chillies and thyme. Cook over a gentle heat until the onion is softened but not browned. Add the stock, bring to the boil, then simmer for about 30 minutes until the vegetables are soft. Remove the chilli and thyme and discard. Blend the soup in a liquidiser or food processor until smooth. Return the soup to a clean pan, bring to the boil and reduce until slightly thickened. Season to taste. Stir in the shrimps or prawns and coconut milk and reheat. Serve hot with finely chopped chilli.

BORTSCH
Serves 6 to 8

The traditional Russian accompaniment to Bortsch is Vatrushky, small slightly sweetened cream cheese tartlets

3 tablespoons oil
450 g/1 lb raw beetroot, peeled and finely diced
2 carrots, peeled and diced
1 turnip, peeled and diced
1 parsnip, peeled and diced
4 celery sticks, chopped
2 onions, chopped
1.75 litres/3 pints chicken stock (see page 4)
juice of 1 lemon
1 teaspoon ground cumin
salt and freshly ground black pepper

garnish
soured cream
black lumpfish roe

Heat the oil in a large saucepan, add the beetroot, carrot, turnip, parsnip, celery and onion. Cook over a gentle heat until the onion is soft but not brown. Add the stock, lemon juice, cumin, salt and pepper. Bring to the boil, then reduce the heat, cover and simmer for about 2 hours. Blend the soup in a liquidiser or food processor until smooth. Return the soup to a clean saucepan, adding more stock if liquid has evaporated during cooking, and reheat. Serve with a swirl of soured cream and a little lumpfish roe on the top. Bortsch can also be served chilled.

BRUSSELS SPROUTS AND CHESTNUT SOUP

Serve 5 to 6

This makes a good autumn soup when Brussels sprouts are plentiful and chestnuts are in the shops.

225 g/8 oz chestnuts
50 g/2 oz butter
1 onion, chopped
2 potatoes, peeled and chopped
**225 g/8 oz Brussels sprouts, trimmed and
  chopped**
900 ml/1½ pints chicken stock (see page 4)
salt and freshly ground black pepper
100 g/4 oz streaky bacon
150 ml/¼ pint single cream

To prepare the chestnuts cut a slit in the skin of each one and cook in boiling water for 4 minutes. Drain and peel off the skin. If the chestnuts cool down and become difficult to peel, reheat them in boiling water for 1 minute.

Melt the butter in a saucepan, add the onion, potatoes, sprouts and chestnuts. Cover the pan and cook gently for about 5 minutes to soften but not brown the vegetables. Stir in the stock, bring to the boil, cover and simmer for about 40 minutes until the vegetables are tender. Blend the soup in a liquidiser or food processor until smooth, season to taste and reheat. Grill the bacon until crisp, then chop. Serve the soup hot, garnished with a swirl of cream and chopped bacon.

STILTON AND CELERY SOUP

Serves 4

A rich soup with a lot of flavour. Cheddar cheese works equally well as Stilton.

50 g/2 oz butter
350 g/12 oz onions, finely chopped
3 celery sticks, finely chopped
50 g/2 oz plain flour
300 ml/½ pint dry cider
300 ml/½ pint milk
350 g/12 oz blue Stilton cheese, crumbled
150 ml/¼ pint single cream
salt and freshly ground black pepper

garnish
celery leaves
puff pastry shapes (see page 6)

Melt the butter in a saucepan. Add the onion and celery and cook gently until soft but not brown, about 10 minutes. Stir in the flour and cook for 1 minute. Remove from the heat and gradually add the cider and the milk, stirring continuously. Bring to the boil, stirring until thickened. Blend the soup in a liquidiser or food processor until smooth, then sieve

to remove any celery fibres. Return the soup to a clean pan. Add the cheese, cover and simmer gently for about 5 minutes until the cheese has melted. Add the cream and reheat but do not boil. Season to taste. Serve hot garnished with celery leaves and puff pastry shapes.

ASPARAGUS SOUP
Serves 4 to 6

Canned asparagus can be used, although the flavour will not be as good. Use a 340-g/12-oz can and use part asparagus liquid and part stock.

225 g/8 oz asparagus
50 g/2 oz butter
1 small onion, chopped
2 tablespoons plain flour
600 ml/1 pint vegetable or chicken stock
  (see page 4)
150 ml/¼ pint single cream
salt and freshly ground black pepper

Wash and trim the asparagus. Remove a few of the tips and reserve for garnish. Chop the asparagus into 2.5-cm/1-inch lengths. Melt the butter in a saucepan, add the onion and asparagus and cook gently until the onion is soft but not browned. Add the flour and cook, stirring, for 1 minute. Gradually add the stock and bring to the boil, cover and simmer for 20 minutes until the asparagus is tender. Blend the soup in a liquidiser or food processor until smooth. Press through a sieve to remove any asparagus fibres and return the soup to a clean saucepan. Stir in the cream and add salt and pepper to taste. Cook the reserved asparagus tips in a little boiling salted water until just tender. Reheat the soup gently, but do not boil. Serve hot garnished with the asparagus tips accompanied by Melba toast (see page 8).

CREAM OF CARROT SOUP
Serves 4 to 6

Carrot and orange are a good combination; try adding the rind and juice of an orange to this soup.

25 g/1 oz butter
1 medium onion, chopped
450 g/1 lb carrots, peeled and chopped
1 large potato, peeled and chopped
900 ml/1½ pints chicken stock (see page 4)
1 bay leaf
salt and freshly ground black pepper
150 ml/¼ pint single cream
1 egg yolk

garnish
chopped fresh herbs, parsley and chives
fried croutons (see page 7)

Melt the butter in a saucepan. Add the onion, carrots and potato, cook over a low heat until the onion is soft but not brown. Add the stock, bay leaf, salt and pepper. Bring to the boil, cover and simmer for about 30 minutes until the vegetables are tender. Remove the bay leaf. Blend the soup in a liquidiser or food processor until smooth. Return the soup to a clean saucepan. Mix together the cream and egg yolk; stir in a little of the soup and blend well. Pour this mixture into the soup and reheat gently, but do not boil. Season to taste. Serve hot sprinkled with herbs and croutons.

WATERCRESS AND ALMOND SOUP
Serves 4 to 6

A quick soup with a luxurious taste. It can also be served chilled—delicious on hot summer days.

25 g/1 oz butter
1 small onion, chopped
100 g/4 oz potato, peeled and chopped
900 ml/1½ pint chicken stock (see page 4)
1 packet or bunch watercress, washed and trimmed
50 g/2 oz ground almonds
150 ml/¼ pint single cream
salt and freshly ground black pepper
150 ml/¼ pint double cream to garnish

Melt the butter in a saucepan, add onion and cook over a low heat until soft but not brown. Add the potato and stock, cover and cook for 20 minutes, until the potato is soft. Add the watercress and cook for a further 5 minutes. Blend in a liquidiser or food processor until smooth and return to a clean saucepan. Stir in the ground almonds and cream, and

season to taste. Reheat soup over a gentle heat, but do not allow to boil. Serve hot, garnished with a swirl of cream, feathered with a cocktail stick (see page 6).

RAJ SOUP
Serves 4 to 6

This mildly curried cauliflower soup goes well with apple and peanuts. For more 'heat' add some chilli powder.

50 g/2 oz butter
2 onions, chopped
450 g/1 lb cauliflower, cut into florets
100 g/4 oz potato, peeled and chopped
1 tablespoon curry paste
900 ml/1½ pints chicken stock (see page 4)
salt and freshly ground black pepper
1 bay leaf
50 g/2 oz creamed coconut

garnish
coriander leaves
apple slices
salted peanuts
shredded coconut

Melt the butter in a large saucepan. Add the onions, cauliflower and potato and cook until the onions are soft but not browned. Add the curry paste and cook, stirring, for 2 minutes. Pour in the stock; add salt and pepper and bay leaf. Bring to boil, cover and simmer for about 30 minutes until the vegetables are tender. Remove the bay leaf. Press the vegetables through a sieve, or blend in a liquidiser or food processor until smooth. Return the soup to a clean pan and gently reheat. Stir in the creamed coconut until dissolved. Taste for seasoning. Serve hot garnished with coriander leaves, and serve bowls of chopped apple, salted peanuts, and shredded coconut separately.

COUNTRY VEGETABLE AND LENTIL SOUP

Serves 6

Delicious served with warm Soda Bread (see page 9)

25 g/1 oz butter
1 large onion, chopped
4 large celery sticks and leaves, roughly
   chopped
2 large carrots, chopped
1 parsnip, chopped
75 g/3 oz split yellow lentils
900 ml/1½ pints vegetable or chicken stock
   (see page 4)
1 bay leaf
2 tablespoons chopped parsley
salt and freshly ground black pepper

Melt the butter in a large saucepan. Add the onion, celery, carrot and parsnip and cook over a low heat for about 10 minutes without browning. Add the split yellow lentils, stock and bay leaf, bring to the boil, cover and simmer for 1-1½ hours until the vegetables and lentils are soft. Remove the bay leaf and blend half the soup in a liquidiser or food processor until smooth and return it to the pan with the remaining soup. This will give a soup with some texture to it. If a smooth soup is preferred, blend all of it. Stir in the parsley, season to taste and reheat. Serve hot.

MUSHROOM SOUP

Serves 4 to 6

Dried mushrooms used in the soup give extra flavour and pungency. They can be bought in health food shops and some supermarkets in this country, or if holidaying in Italy or France why not bring some back? If not using dried mushrooms, increase the fresh mushrooms to 450g/1 lb.

50 g/2 oz butter
1 small onion, chopped
350 g/12 oz small flat mushrooms
1 clove garlic, crushed
1 tablespoon plain flour
900 ml/1½ pints vegetable or chicken stock
   (see page 4)
25 g/1 oz dried mushrooms
150 ml/¼ pint single cream
salt and freshly ground black pepper
pinch of grated nutmeg

Melt the butter in a saucepan. Add the onion and fresh mushrooms and cook gently until the onion is soft but not browned. Add the garlic and flour and cook, stirring, for 1 minute. Gradually stir in the stock, add the dried mushrooms, cover and simmer for 15-20 minutes until mushrooms are tender. Blend in a liquidiser or food processor until smooth. Stir in the cream, salt, pepper and nutmeg to taste. Gently reheat but do not boil. Serve with hot garlic bread (see page 8).

LEEK AND POTATO SOUP
Serves 4 to 6

An ideal start to a traditional Sunday lunch.

25 g/1 oz butter
450 g/1 lb leeks, sliced and washed
1 medium onion, chopped
350 g/12 oz potatoes, peeled and diced
1.15 litres/2 pints chicken or vegetable stock
   (see page 4)
salt and freshly ground black pepper

Melt the butter in a saucepan. Add the leeks, onion and potatoes and cook gently for about 5 minutes until the onion is soft but not browned. Stir in the stock, salt and pepper, bring to the boil, cover and simmer for about 45 minutes until the vegetables are soft. Blend in a liquidiser or food processor until smooth. Return the soup to a clean saucepan, season to taste and reheat. Serve with Cheese and Carrot Soda Bread (see page 9), or Bacon Rolls (see page 6).

To make Crème Vichyssoise, stir in 150 ml/¼ pint single cream after puréeing the soup. Chill. Sprinkle with chives before serving.

MAIN MEAL SOUPS

PROVENCAL FISH SOUP
Serves 4

1 tablespoon olive oil
1 onion, finely chopped
2 cloves garlic, crushed
397-g/14-oz can tomatoes
300 ml/½ pint fish stock (see page 4)
1 bay leaf
100 g/4 oz long-grain rice
225 g/8 oz monk fish or cod, skinned, boned
  and cut into chunks
175 g/6 oz cooked mussels, thawed if frozen
100 g/4 oz peeled cooked prawns
2 tablespoons chopped parsley
salt and freshly ground black pepper

garnish
unpeeled cooked prawns
mussels in their shells
4 tablespoons single cream

Heat the oil in a large saucepan, add the onion and cook until soft but not browned. Add the garlic, tomatoes and their juice, fish stock, bay leaf and rice. Bring to the boil, cover and simmer for about 10 minutes until the rice is almost cooked. Add the monk fish and simmer for a further 5 minutes. Add the mussels and prawns and simmer for a further 5 minutes. Finally stir in the parsley, salt and pepper. Garnish with unpeeled prawns and mussels in their shells and top with a spoonful of cream. Serve with plenty of crusty bread to mop up the juices.

MINESTRONE
Serves 6

Don't be put off by the long list of ingredients. Other vegetables can be substituted according to what you have, but keep the overall quantity the same.

3 tablespoons olive oil
1 celery stick, thinly sliced
1 onion, finely chopped
1 large carrot, diced
1 turnip, peeled and cut into matchstick-sized
  pieces
1 medium potato, peeled and diced
1 small leek, washed and shredded
1 clove garlic, crushed
2 rashers rindless unsmoked streaky bacon,
  chopped
1.15 litres/2 pints chicken or vegetable stock
  (see page 4)
2 teaspoons chopped fresh sage
salt and freshly ground black pepper
225 g/8 oz cabbage, shredded
75 g/3 oz small pasta shapes
225 g/8 oz canned tomatoes, chopped
3 tablespoons frozen peas
100 g/4 oz runner beans or French beans, cut
  into 1-cm/½-inch pieces
grated Parmesan cheese

Heat the oil in a large saucepan. Add the celery, onion, carrot and turnip and cook gently until the onion is soft but not browned. Add the potato, leek, garlic and bacon and cook for a further 5 minutes. Pour in the stock; add the sage, salt and pepper; bring to the boil; cover and simmer for 45 minutes. Add the cabbage, pasta, tomatoes, peas and beans. Cover and simmer for a further 15 minutes until the pasta and cabbage are cooked. Taste for seasoning. Serve hot with grated Parmesan cheese served separately.

AVGOLEMONO
Serves 6

This soup is traditionally served by Cypriots and Greeks on Easter morning to end the fasting in celebration of the resurrection of Christ.

1.5 kg/3 lb chicken
1.75 litres/3 pints water
150 g/6 oz long-grain rice
4 eggs
juice of 4 lemons
salt and freshly ground black pepper
lemon slices to garnish

Place the chicken in a large saucepan with the water. Bring to the boil, cover and simmer for about 1½ hours until the meat falls from the carcass. Skim off any scum from time to time. Keep the chicken warm whilst finishing the soup. Add the rice to the stock in the pan, bring to the boil and simmer for 10-15 minutes until the rice is cooked. Beat the eggs with the lemon juice, salt and pepper. Gradually add some of the stock to the eggs, stirring well. When about 600 ml/1 pint of stock has been added, strain it back into the saucepan. Reheat gently but do not allow it to boil, otherwise the eggs will curdle. Serve hot garnished with lemon slices, with the chicken served separately.

BACON AND LENTIL SOUP

Serves 4 to 6

Taste this soup before adding extra salt. The bacon will probably provide sufficient.

900 g/2 lb bacon knuckle
225 g/8 oz orange lentils
1 large onion, finely chopped
1 large carrot, peeled and diced
2 celery sticks, sliced
1 sprig parsley
salt and freshly ground black pepper
2 large tomatoes

Soak the bacon joint in cold water overnight. Drain the bacon and discard the soaking water. Place the bacon joint and lentils in a large saucepan with 1.75 litres/3 pints of water. Bring to the boil, cover and simmer for 1 hour. Add the onion, carrot, celery, parsley and pepper. Simmer for about 30 minutes. Remove the bacon joint, cut off the meat and chop it into bite-sized pieces. Return the meat to the soup and discard the bone. Cut a cross in the base of each tomato and dip into boiling water for 30 seconds. Peel off the skin, cut into quarters, remove the skin and chop the flesh. Stir into the soup and reheat. Sprinkle with extra chopped parsley, if liked, and serve with Tomato Herb Soda Bread (see page 9).

POT AU FEU
Serves 6

This lovely rustic French country soup makes a meal in itself.

1 kg/2 lb shin of beef with bones
2 teaspoons salt
1 teaspoon freshly ground black pepper
1 onion, quartered
1 bouquet garni
1 clove garlic, finely chopped
1 carrot, peeled and quartered
1 turnip, peeled and quartered
2 leeks, washed and sliced
500 g/1 lb potatoes, peeled and diced
500 g/1 lb white cabbage, thickly sliced
chopped parsley to garnish

Trim any excess fat from the meat and discard. Place the meat in a large saucepan and cover with water. Add the salt and slowly bring to the boil. Skim off any scum. Reduce the heat; add the pepper, onion, bouquet garni and garlic. Half cover the pan and simmer gently for about 2 hours, adding more water if necessary.

Remove the bones and bouquet garni. Add the carrot, turnip, leeks, potatoes and cabbage. Simmer gently for a further hour. Skim to remove any fat and bring to the boil again just before serving. Taste for seasoning and adjust if necessary. Sprinkle with chopped parsley. The meat can be served separately or chopped and served in the soup.

GOULASH SOUP
Serves 6

Minced beef can be used instead of stewing steak in this soup. Reduce simmering time to 30 minutes.

1 tablespoon oil
2 onions, finely chopped
225 g/8 oz stewing steak, cut into small strips
1 clove garlic, crushed
1 red pepper, seeded and finely chopped
1 green pepper, seeded and finely chopped
1 tablespoon paprika
2 tablespoons plain flour
396-g/14-oz can tomatoes, chopped
1.15 litres/2 pints beef stock (see page 4)
salt and freshly ground black pepper
1 quantity Herb Dumplings (see page 8)

garnish
6 tablespoons soured cream
paprika

Heat the oil in a large saucepan. Add the onions and cook gently until soft but not browned. Add the meat, garlic, red and green pepper and cook for 5 minutes. Add the paprika and flour and cook for 2 minutes, stirring. Add the tomatoes with their juice and the stock. Bring to the boil, cover and simmer for 1 hour until the meat is tender. Season to taste.

Make the dumplings following the method on page 8 and shape into 18 small balls. Add to the soup, cover and simmer for 10 minutes. Serve hot with a spoonful of soured cream on the top lightly sprinkled with paprika.

CHILLED SOUPS

GAZPACHO
Serves 6

A quick soup with a punchy flavour.

1 thick slice white bread, crusts removed
2 tablespoons wine vinegar
450 g/1 lb ripe tomatoes
1 large Spanish onion, chopped
½ cucumber, peeled and chopped
300 ml/½ pint tomato juice
1 clove garlic, peeled and chopped
1 green pepper, seeded and chopped
600 ml/1 pint cold chicken stock (see page 4)
2 tablespoons olive oil
salt and freshly ground black pepper

garnish
green pepper, seeded and finely diced
fried croutons (see page 7)
cucumber, finely diced

Soak the bread in the wine vinegar for a few minutes. Cut a cross in the base of each tomato and dip into boiling water for 30 seconds. Peel off the skin, cut into quarters, remove the seeds and chop the flesh. Place the soaked bread, tomatoes, onion, cucumber, tomato juice, garlic and green pepper in a liquidiser or food processor and blend until smooth. Transfer the purée to a bowl and beat in the stock and olive oil. Season to taste and chill. Serve well chilled accompanied by the diced green pepper, croutons and cucumber in separate bowls.

BLACK CHERRY SOUP
Serves 6

This chilled soup makes an unusual start to a meal.

900 g/2 lb black cherries, fresh or frozen
1.15 litres/2 pints water
1 stick cinnamon
100 g/4 oz caster sugar
1 tablespoon cornflour
150 ml/¼ pint sweet white wine

garnish
4 tablespoons double cream
15 g/½ oz toasted flaked almonds

Place the cherries, water and cinnamon in a saucepan. Bring to the boil, reduce the heat, cover and simmer for 25 minutes. Push the cherries through a sieve into a clean saucepan and discard the stones and cinnamon stick. Mix the cornflour with a little water to make a smooth paste and stir into the soup with the sugar. Bring to the boil, stirring, until slightly thickened. Stir in the wine and chill. Serve with a swirl of cream on the top, feathered with a cocktail stick (see page 6) and sprinkle with toasted flaked almonds.

CUCUMBER AND MINT SOUP
Serves 4

This simple and refreshing soup requires no cooking and takes only a few minutes to make. If fresh mint is not available, use 1 teaspoon of dried mint and garnish with thin slices of cucumber.

6 spring onions
1 clove garlic, crushed
1 large cucumber, chopped
4 fresh mint leaves
450 ml/¾ pint cold chicken stock (see page 4)
150 ml/¼ pint natural yogurt
salt and freshly ground black pepper
fresh mint sprigs to garnish

Place the spring onions, garlic, cucumber and mint in a liquidiser or food processor and blend until smooth. Add the stock, yogurt, salt and pepper and blend until well mixed. Pour into individual serving bowls and chill. Add two ice cubes to each bowl just before serving and garnish with fresh mint.

NO-COOK STARTERS

These ideas for quick, simple starters which require no cooking rely on colourful combinations of fresh ingredients. They are ideal when time is short or when extra people are invited and the main course and dessert need to be stretched further. Adding an extra course is an easy way to solve the problem. Presentation is important. Even a selection of meats and salamis bought from the delicatessen can provide an eye-catching first course if arranged attractively on plates with salad garnish and a few gherkins and olives.

Crudités

Crudités are a selection of raw vegetables, prepared and ready to eat. They provide a colourful platter for an informal starter which can be eaten with pre-dinner drinks before sitting at the dining table. They can be served on their own or with a dip or selection of dips (see pages 27-29). The vegetables can be prepared a few hours ahead, wrapped in cling film and kept in the refrigerator until required. Choose a colourful selection from the vegetables below:

Carrots—peel and cut into chunky sticks.
Spring onions—trim and split in half lengthways if large.
Cauliflower—cut into florets.
Celery—trim and cut into 7.5-cm/3-inch lengths, keep the leaves on inner sticks.
Fennel—cut into wedges and brush with lemon juice.

Cherry tomatoes—leave the calyx on to hold the tomato when 'dipping'.
Button mushrooms—trim the stalks, then wipe with damp absorbent kitchen paper and brush with lemon juice.
Green, red and yellow pepper—remove the core and seeds, cut into thin strips lengthways.
Radishes—trim and halve if large.
Chicory—separate the leaves and trim the base.
Cucumber—cut into chunky sticks.

Dips

As well as crudités, crisps, bread sticks, tortilla chips, poppadums, and strips of warm pitta bread also make good 'dippers'.

TOMATO GARLIC DIP
makes about 300 ml/½ pint

75 g/3 oz fresh white bread crumbs
4 tablespoons tomato relish
1 tablespoon tomato ketchup
150 ml/¼ pint soured cream
3 tablespoons mayonnaise
1 tablespoon lemon juice
1 tablespoon Worcestershire sauce
1 clove garlic, crushed
salt and pepper

Mix all the ingredients together thoroughly. Cover and chill for 2 hours to allow flavours to develop.

AIOLI
makes just over 150 ml/¼ pint

This is garlic mayonnaise. Sunflower oil can replace half the olive oil if preferred. Use an electric hand whisk, liquidiser or food processor for best results.

1 egg yolk
¼ teaspoon made mustard
2 cloves garlic, crushed
1 tablespoon lemon juice
salt and freshly ground black pepper
150 ml/¼ pint olive oil
1 tablespoon boiling water

Beat together the egg yolk, mustard, garlic, salt and pepper and half the lemon juice. Gradually add half the oil, beating continuously, until the mixture thickens. Beat in the remaining lemon juice, followed by the remaining oil in a thin stream. Finally stir in the boiling water and taste for seasoning. This will keep in a covered container in the refrigerator for about 2 weeks.

BLUE CHEESE DIP
makes about 300 ml/½ pint

125 g/5 oz Danish blue or Stilton cheese
150 ml/¼ pint strained Greek yogurt
2 tablespoons double cream

Mash the cheese with a fork. Gradually beat in the yoghurt, then stir in the cream. Chill for 2 hours before serving.

CHESHIRE CIDER DIP
makes about 300 ml/½ pint

This dip is particularly good with slices of Cox's apple. Dip them in lemon juice to prevent them browning.

350 g/12 oz Cheshire cheese, finely grated
150 ml/¼ pint medium sweet cider
salt and freshly ground black pepper

Place the cheese in a food processor. Gradually add the cider and blend until smooth. Season to taste with salt and pepper. Cover and chill for about 2 hours before serving.

GUACAMOLE
Serves 4 to 6

If made too far in advance Guacamole can start to discolour.

2 ripe avocados
1 tomato, peeled and chopped
2 tablespoons lemon juice
1 clove garlic, crushed
½ teaspoon chilli powder or to taste
salt to taste
3 spring onions, finely chopped
½ small red pepper, seeded and finely chopped

Cut the avocados in half, remove the stones and peel. Mash the avocados in a bowl with the tomato, lemon juice, garlic, chilli powder and salt to taste. Stir in the spring onions. Reserve some of the red pepper for garnish and stir the remainder into the dip. Spoon into a bowl and sprinkle with reserved red pepper. To make in a blender or food processor, reserve some red pepper for garnish and blend the remaining ingredients until smooth. Pile into a bowl and garnish. Guacamole is best when served within one hour of making. Serve with tortilla chips, crisps or raw vegetables.

TARAMASALATA
Serves 4 to 6

Although Taramasalata is now widely available in supermarkets, much of it is bright pink and bears little resemblance to the real thing.

175 g/6 oz smoked cod's roe
175 g/6 oz fresh white bread, crusts removed
4 tablespoons milk
freshly ground black pepper
1 clove garlic, crushed
150 ml/¼ pint oil
2 tablespoons lemon juice

Remove the skin from the cod's roe and place the roe in a bowl. Soak the bread in the milk and mash well with a fork. Squeeze out the surplus liquid and place the bread in a bowl with the cod's roe. Add the pepper and garlic and mix well. Gradually beat in the oil, a little at a time, and then beat in the lemon juice. Taste for seasoning and transfer to a serving bowl. Cover and chill before serving. Serve with warmed pitta bread or hot toast and black olives.

HUMMUS
Serves 4 to 6

Dried chickpeas can be used, but must be soaked overnight and then boiled for about 2 hours until soft. Use about 175 g/6 oz dried chickpeas.

432-g/15-oz can chickpeas
2 cloves garlic, crushed
4 tablespoons tahini
4 tablespoons lemon juice
salt and freshly ground black pepper
1 tablespoon olive oil

garnish
paprika
fresh coriander leaves

Drain the chickpeas and reserve the liquid. Mash the chickpeas with a fork or purée in a food processor. Beat in the crushed garlic, tahini and lemon juice until well blended. Taste for seasoning and beat in the olive oil. The mixture should be fairly soft. If it is too thick, beat in a little of the reserved chickpea liquid. Cover and chill until required. Serve in a bowl sprinkled with paprika and garnished with coriander leaves. Serve with warm pitta bread.

GRAVADLAX

Serves 6 to 8

Although there is no cooking involved with this starter, it does require forward planning

675-g/1½-lb piece middle-cut fresh salmon
2 tablespoons coarse sea salt
4 teaspoons caster sugar
1 teaspoon black peppercorns, crushed
bunch fresh dill, chopped

garnish
fresh dill
lemon wedges

Wash the piece of salmon and dry it with absorbent kitchen paper. Skin the fish and remove the bones to make 2 fillets. Mix together the salt, sugar and pepper and rub over both sides of each fillet. Place one-third of the dill in a shallow dish and cover with one of the salmon fillets. Sprinkle another third of the dill over the salmon fillet and cover with the other salmon fillet. Sprinkle the remaining dill over the top. Cover with cling film and a plate or board weighted down. Chill for about 36 hours.

To serve, slice the salmon thinly across the grain. Garnish with fresh dill and lemon wedges. Serve with thin slices of buttered wholemeal or rye bread.

CEVICHE

Serves 4 to 6

Ceviche is a Mexican dish. Like Gravadlax the fish is not cooked, but it does need time to marinate. Lemon juice can be used if limes are not available.

450 g/1 lb fresh cod or haddock
juice of 2 limes
1 small onion, sliced
1 tomato, peeled, seeds removed, chopped
113-g/4-oz can green chillies, chopped
3 tablespoons vegetable oil
1 tablespoon wine vinegar
salt and pepper

Skin the fish, remove any bones and cut the flesh into cubes. In a non-metal container mix together the fish and lime juice; cover and chill overnight. When ready, the fish will be opaque as though it has been cooked. Drain the fish, mix with the remaining ingredients and serve chilled.

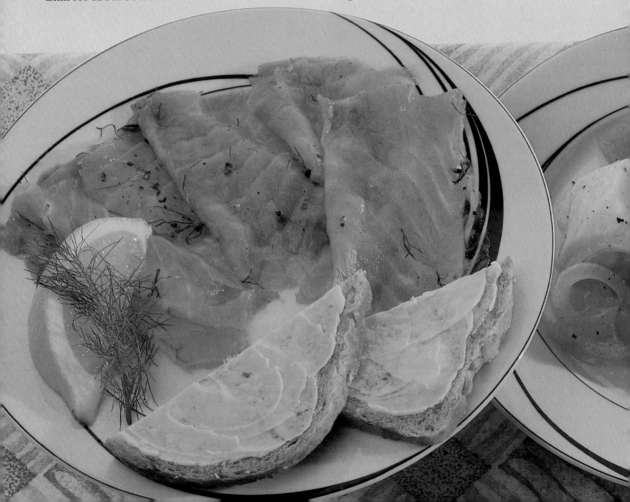

PRAWN COCKTAIL
Serves 4

One of the most popular starters of all time. It is served here in tomato cups, but can be served on scallop shells or in glasses if preferred.

4 large tomatoes
½ small lettuce
175 g/6 oz peeled cooked prawns

dressing
150 ml/¼ pint thick mayonnaise
2 teaspoons lemon juice
1 tablespoon tomato purée
2 teaspoons Worcestershire sauce
salt and freshly ground black
  pepper

garnish
cayenne
4 unpeeled cooked prawns
4 wedges lemon or lime

Cut a slice off the top of each tomato and hollow out the centres. Wash, dry and shred the lettuce and divide between the tomatoes. Mix all the dressing ingredients together. Place the prawns on top of the lettuce and spoon the sauce over the top. Sprinkle with cayenne and garnish with unpeeled prawns and lemon or lime.

For variety use a mixture of shellfish, such as mussels, cockles, crab and prawns, or a mixture of cooked seafood, such as monk fish, squid and shellfish.

TOMATO AND MOZZARELLA SALAD
Serves 4

A mixture of parsley and chives makes a good alternative to basil.

3 large beefsteak tomatoes, sliced
175 g/6 oz mozzarella cheese, drained and cubed

dressing
6 tablespoons wine vinegar
1 tablespoon chopped fresh basil or 1 teaspoon dried basil
salt and freshly ground black pepper
pinch of sugar
2 tablespoons olive oil
fresh basil leaves or coriander to garnish

Arrange the tomato slices on small plates with the mozzarella. To make the dressing, combine the wine vinegar with the basil, salt and pepper and sugar. Beat in the oil until the dressing thickens. Pour the dressing over the salads. Cover and leave for about 1 hour for the tomato and cheese to soak up the dressing. Just before serving, garnish with fresh basil leaves or coriander if available.

AVOCADO WITH ORANGE
Serves 4

Once cut, avocados discolour and blacken, just like an apple or banana, but this can be delayed by dipping in lemon juice. The oranges can be prepared in advance and covered, ready to be combined with the avocado at the last minute.

2 oranges
2 ripe avocados
2 tablespoons lemon juice
50 g/2 oz pecan or walnut halves

dressing
2 tablespoons unsweetened orange juice
1 teaspoon lemon juice
salt and freshly ground black pepper
4 tablespoons sunflower oil

Cut a slice off the top and bottom of each orange. Using a sharp knife, working around the orange, cut downwards to remove the peel and white pith. Holding the orange in one hand, carefully cut out and remove the segments from the membranes. Cut the avocados in half and remove the stones; dip the cut surfaces in lemon juice. Peel off the skin and slice the avocados and dip them in lemon juice. Arrange the orange and avocado on small plates with the pecan or walnuts. To make the dressing, combine the orange juice, lemon juice, salt and pepper. Beat in the oil until the dressing thickens. Pour over the salads and serve.

FETA AND OLIVE SALAD
Serves 6

Both feta cheese and anchovies are rather salty, so do not add too much salt to the dressing.

1 small cos lettuce
½ cucumber, sliced
2 tomatoes, cut into wedges
175 g/6 oz pitted black olives
100 g/4 oz feta cheese, crumbled
50-g/2-oz can anchovy fillets, drained
dressing
2 tablespoons red wine vinegar
1 teaspoon dried oregano
salt and freshly ground black pepper
½ clove garlic
6 tablespoons olive oil

Wash and dry the lettuce leaves. Place them in a salad bowl with the cucumber, tomatoes, black olives and feta cheese. To make the dressing, combine the red wine vinegar with the oregano, salt and pepper and garlic. Beat in the olive oil until the dressing thickens. Just before serving, toss the salad in the dressing and arrange anchovy fillets on the top. Serve with warmed pitta bread.

MELON MINT AND PINEAPPLE COCKTAIL
Serves 4

A small can of pineapple pieces in natural juice can be used instead of fresh pineapple.

1 medium-sized honeydew melon
½ small pineapple
2 teaspoons caster sugar
1 tablespoon sherry
2 tablespoons chopped fresh mint

garnish
fresh mint
maraschino cherries
wedges of fresh pineapple

Cut the melon in half, scoop out the seeds and cut the flesh into cubes. Cut the pineapple into wedges, removing the core and cutting off the skin and the 'eyes'. Mix together the melon, pineapple, caster sugar, sherry and mint. Spoon into glasses or small bowls and chill. Garnish with a wedge of fresh pineapple, a sprig of fresh mint and a cherry.

MELON IN PORT
Serves 4

A refreshing starter, ideal for preceding a filling main course.

2 ripe charentais melons
2 tablespoons soft brown sugar
8 tablespoons port
demerara sugar

Cut the melons in half and serrate the edges. Scoop out and discard the seeds. Mix together the brown sugar and port and spoon into the melon halves. Sprinkle the edges with demerara sugar. Chill before serving.

For variety, use honeydew melon, cutting the flesh into cubes and serving in glasses, or use sweet vermouth instead of port.

FRUIT 'N' HAM PLATTERS
Serves 4

A refreshing, simple starter. Strawberries make a good addition when in season.

2 pink grapefruits
2 kiwi fruits, peeled and sliced
175 g/6 oz Parma ham, thinly sliced

Cut a slice off the top and bottom of the grapefruits. Using a sharp knife and working around the grapefruits, cut downwards to remove the peel and white pith. Holding a grapefruit in one hand, carefully cut out and remove the segments from the membranes. Repeat with the other grapefruit. Arrange in shallow dishes with slices of kiwi fruit and Parma ham. Serve chilled.

COLD STARTERS

Most of these starters can be prepared in advance with the minimum of last minute garnishing required. They include pâtés, mousses and salads suitable for serving all year round.

FARMHOUSE PÂTÉ
Serves 6 to 8

This coarse pâté is ideal for an informal meal.

225 g/8 oz unsmoked streaky bacon rashers
225 g/8 oz pig's liver
1 small onion
1 clove garlic
225 g/8 oz shoulder of pork
225 g/8 oz pork sausage
½ teaspoon dried marjoram or mixed herbs
salt and freshly ground black pepper

Remove the rinds from the bacon and stretch the rashers using the blade of a knife. Line a 450-g/1-lb loaf tin with the bacon rashers.

Cut out any membranes from the liver; then mince the liver with the onion, garlic and shoulder of pork. Stir in the sausage meat, marjoram or dried herbs, salt and pepper. Put the mixture in the bacon-lined tin, level the surface and cover with foil. Stand in a roasting tin half full of water. Cook in a moderate oven (180°C, 350°F, gas 4) for 2 hours. Drain off any liquid around the pâté. Stand a plate or board on top of the foil and weight down. Allow to cool, then chill in the refrigerator overnight. Turn out and serve sliced with toast or French bread and salad garnish.

CHICKEN LIVER PÂTÉ
Serves 4

Try adding a tablespoon of brandy before stirring in the cream for an extra dash of luxury. The mixture may seem rather sloppy, but it will firm up as it chills.

225 g/8 oz chicken livers
50 g/2 oz butter
1 small onion, chopped
1 clove garlic, crushed
salt and freshly ground black pepper
2 tablespoons single cream

Rinse the chicken livers and pat dry with absorbent kitchen paper; trim them using kitchen scissors. Melt the butter in a frying pan. Add the onion, garlic and chicken livers and cook gently until the onion is soft and the chicken livers are just cooked. Cool slightly. Mince the mixture or purée it in a liquidiser or food processor with salt and pepper. Stir in the cream. Transfer the mixture to a serving dish. Cover and chill. Serve with hot buttered fingers of toast or crusty bread.

SMOKED SALMON PÂTÉ
Serves 4

Ask your fishmonger or delicatessen for smoked salmon trimmings for this recipe. They are cheaper than slices.

100 g/4 oz unsalted butter
100 g/4 oz smoked salmon trimmings
freshly ground black pepper
¼ teaspoon paprika
2 teaspoons lemon juice

Melt the butter and pour it into a liquidiser or food processor. Add the remaining ingredients and blend until smooth. Transfer mixture to a serving dish and allow to set. In warm weather chill in the refrigerator; in cold weather it will set in a cool kitchen. Serve with wedges of lemon and hot toast, crusty bread or crackers.

KIPPER PÂTÉ
Serves 5 to 6

Boil-in-the-bag kipper fillets are used to retain all the flavour during cooking. If using fresh or frozen kipper fillets, cook in a frying pan with a little butter.

200-g/7-oz packet frozen boil-in-the-bag
  kipper fillets
25 g/1 oz fresh bread crumbs
150 g/6 oz low-fat soft cheese
2 tablespoons natural yoghurt
1 tablespoon lemon juice
pinch of cayenne
parsley to garnish

Cook the kipper fillets following the instructions on the packet. Allow to cool slightly. Remove the skin and larger bones from the kippers and place the flesh in a mixing bowl or food processor. If mixing by hand, break up the fish with a fork, add remaining ingredients and beat with a wooden spoon until well blended. If using a food processor, blend all the ingredients together until smooth. Taste for seasoning and add more cayenne or lemon juice if necessary. Spoon the mixture into a serving dish or individual dishes. Cover and chill for at least 1 hour to allow flavours to develop. Before serving, sprinkle a little cayenne on top and garnish with parsley. Serve with fingers of wholemeal toast or pitta bread and lemon wedges.

LAYERED FISH TERRINE

Serves 4 to 6

The watercress sauce served with the terrine contrasts well with the white and pink layers of fish.

white layer
225 g/8 oz haddock fillets, skinned and boned
200 ml/7 fl oz double cream
salt and white pepper
1 egg yolk
2 egg whites

pink layer
175 g/6 oz peeled cooked prawns
50 g/2 oz skimmed milk soft cheese
1 egg, beaten
salt and freshly ground black pepper
1 tablespoon tomato purée

watercress sauce
½ bunch watercress, trimmed and washed
150 ml/¼ pint single cream
salt and freshly ground pepper
unpeeled prawns to garnish

Grease a 450-g/1-lb loaf tin. For the white layer, mince the haddock and mix with the cream, salt and pepper and egg yolk. Whisk the egg whites until just stiff, then carefully fold into the fish mixture using a metal spoon.

For the pink layer, mince the prawns; then mix them with the soft cheese, egg, salt and pepper and tomato purée.

Spoon half the white mixture into the loaf tin and level the surface. Top with the prawn mixture, then cover with the remaining white fish mixture. Cover with greased foil and stand in a roasting tin half full of hot water. Cook in a preheated moderate oven (180°C, 350°F, gas 4) for about 40 minutes or until firm to the touch. Pour off any juices from the tin and reserve for the sauce. Allow to cool.

Blend the watercress, cream and reserved juices together in a liquidiser or food processor until smooth. Season to taste. When the terrine is cool, unmould it onto a serving plate and serve sliced with watercress sauce.

SPRING VEGETABLE TERRINE

Serves 4

This stunning starter is not as complicated to make as it looks.

175 g/6 oz fresh spinach
175 g/6 oz baby carrots, scraped
50 g/2 oz French beans, trimmed
2 eggs
salt and freshly ground black pepper
½ teaspoon grated nutmeg
150 ml/¼ pint single cream
4 tablespoons grated Parmesan cheese
1 tablespoon lemon juice
450 g/1 lb potatoes, freshly cooked and puréed

Cut out and discard any coarse stalks from the spinach. Wash the leaves and cook them in boiling salted water for about 30 seconds. Drain. Line a greased 450-g/1-lb loaf tin evenly with the spinach allowing some spinach to hang over the edge. Reserve 3 or 4 leaves for the top.

Cut the carrots into strips a similar length and size as the beans. Lightly cook both vegetables in boiling salted water for 3-4 minutes. Drain.

Beat the eggs, salt and pepper, nutmeg, cream, Parmesan and lemon juice into the potato. Spoon one-quarter of the potato into the base of the spinach-lined tin and arrange half the carrots in lines lengthways on top. Cover with another quarter of the potato mixture and arrange beans in the same way on top. Repeat with another quarter of potato and remaining carrots. Finish with remaining potato. Fold the overhanging spinach leaves over the potato and cover with reserved leaves. Cover with foil and place in a roasting tin half-filled with hot water. Cook in a pre-heated moderate oven (180°C, 350°F, gas 4) for about 50 minutes, remove the foil and return to the oven for a further 15 minutes until firm to the touch. Let cool, then unmould onto a serving dish. Serve sliced, cool but not chilled.

AVOCADO MOUSSE
Serves 6 to 8

A creamy mousse with a subtle flavour.

4 teaspoons gelatine
150 ml/¼ pint chicken stock (see page 4)
3 large ripe avocados
2 spring onions, chopped
2 tablespoons lemon juice
salt and freshly ground black pepper
150 ml/¼ pint mayonnaise
300 ml/½ pint double cream

garnish
1 small avocado
lemon juice
unpeeled cooked prawns

Dissolve the gelatine in 4 tablespoons hot water over a pan of simmering water. Add the chicken stock and cool slightly. Blend the flesh of the avocados in a blender or food processor with the spring onions, lemon juice and seasoning. When the mixture is smooth, pour in the gelatine stock and blend again. Transfer the mixture to a bowl and fold in the mayonnaise. Whip the double cream until it just holds its shape and lightly fold into the avocado mixture. Pour into an oiled 2-litre/3½-pint ring mould. Cover with cling film and chill overnight in the refrigerator.

To serve, dip the mould into hot water for about 10 seconds and invert onto a serving plate. If the mousse does not come out, loosen the edge with a sharp knife and quickly dip in hot water again. Garnish with whole prawns and slices of avocado dipped in lemon juice. Serve sliced, with brown bread and butter.

SALMON MOUSSE
Serves 6

Always sprinkle gelatine onto the liquid and not the other way round.

25 g/1 oz butter
25 g/1 oz plain flour
250 ml/½ pint milk
4 teaspoons gelatine
2 eggs, separated
198-g/7-oz can pink salmon
2 tablespoons tomato purée
grated rind and juice of 1 lemon
2 tablespoons dry sherry
salt and freshly ground black pepper
125 ml/¼ pint double cream

garnish
cucumber slices
watercress or curly
**   endive lettuce**

Lightly oil a 900-ml/1½-pint ring mould or fish mould. Melt the butter in a saucepan, add the flour and cook, stirring for 1 minute. Remove from the heat and gradually add the milk. Return to the heat, bring to the boil, stirring until thickened. Cover with damp greaseproof paper and allow to cool slightly. Dissolve the gelatine in 3 tablespoons hot water over a pan of simmering water. Beat into the white sauce with the egg yolks and leave until on the point of setting. Drain the salmon and mash with the tomato purée, lemon rind and juice, sherry, salt and pepper. Mix well. Lightly whip the cream. Stir the salmon mixture into the white sauce and fold in the cream. Whisk the egg whites until just stiff and carefully fold into the salmon mixture using a metal spoon. Pour into the prepared mould and allow to set in the refrigerator.

To serve, dip the mould into hot water for 30 seconds and invert onto serving plate. Garnish with halved cucumber slices and watercress or curly endive lettuce. Serve with Melba toast (see page 8).

TOMATO MOUSSE
Serves 6

This piquant flavoured mousse can also be set in a 900-ml/1½-pint ring mould and the centre filled with egg mayonnaise.

3 teaspoons gelatine
2 tablespoons lemon juice
600 ml/1 pint tomato juice
1 small clove garlic, crushed
1 teaspoon sugar
½ teaspoon Tabasco sauce
salt and freshly ground black pepper
150 ml/¼ pint chicken stock (see page 4)
1 egg white

garnish
stuffed green olives, sliced
celery

Dissolve the gelatine in the lemon juice over a pan of simmering water. Heat the tomato juice with the garlic, sugar, Tabasco sauce, salt and pepper and chicken stock until well combined. Add the gelatine and allow the mixture to cool until just beginning to thicken. Whisk the egg white until just stiff and fold into the tomato mixture. Pour into six oiled 150-ml/¼-pint moulds or ramekin dishes. Chill until set. To serve, dip the moulds into hot water for about 10 seconds and invert onto small serving plates. Serve garnished with slices of stuffed green olives and sticks of celery.

STUFFED EGGS
Serves 6

Boil the eggs on the day of serving to avoid a black ring around the yolk. Pricking the blunt end of the eggs with a pin or egg pricker helps to stop eggs cracking whilst boiling.

9 eggs, size 2

prawn filling
25 g/1 oz peeled cooked prawns, chopped
1 tablespoon mayonnaise
1 teaspoon lemon juice
salt and freshly ground black pepper
1 tablespoon tomato ketchup

watercress filling
2 tablespoons finely chopped watercress
2 tablespoons natural yoghurt
25 g/1 oz herb and garlic soft cheese

olive and gherkin filling
1 gherkin, finely chopped
1 tablespoon mayonnaise
3 stuffed green olives, chopped
salt and freshly ground black pepper

garnish
lettuce
stuffed green olives
watercress
unpeeled cooked prawns

Place the eggs in a saucepan of cold water. Bring to the boil and simmer for 10 minutes. Cool under running cold water and shell the eggs. Cut in half, scoop out the yolks and divide them between 3 small bowls. Add the prawn filling ingredients to one bowl and mix well. Add the watercress filling ingredients to another bowl and mix well. Add the olive and

gherkin filling to the remaining bowl and combine thoroughly. Spoon or pipe the fillings back into the whites. Place one stuffed egg of each filling on small serving plates and garnish with lettuce, stuffed green olives, watercress and prawns.

BACON, AVOCADO AND ORANGE SALAD
Serves 4

To test an avocado for ripeness, gently press the thin end with the thumbs. It should feel slightly soft.

6 rashers rindless streaky bacon
1 ripe avocado
1 tablespoon lemon juice
100 g/4 oz cooked long-grain rice
4 spring onions, finely chopped
50 g/2 oz walnuts, chopped
1 orange, peeled and sliced

dressing
4 tablespoons orange juice
2 teaspoons lemon juice
2 tablespoons olive oil
salt and freshly ground black pepper

Grill the bacon until crisp, and roughly chop. Peel and slice the avocado and sprinkle with lemon juice. Mix together the salad ingredients except the bacon. Mix together the dressing ingredients and toss the salad. Spoon into individual bowls and sprinkle with bacon pieces. Serve within 30 minutes of making; otherwise the avocado will start to brown.

SALAD NICOISE
Serves 4

Tuna in brine is now widely available. It has less calories than tuna in oil.

175 g/6 oz French beans, trimmed
196-g/7-oz can tuna, drained
1 crisp lettuce, cut into wedges
1 small onion, thinly sliced
4 tomatoes, quartered
2 hard-boiled eggs, quartered
8 black olives
50-g/2-oz can anchovy fillets, drained

dressing
1 tablespoon white wine vinegar
3 tablespoons olive oil
salt and freshly ground black pepper
½ clove garlic, crushed

Cook the beans in boiling salted water for about 4 minutes until just tender. Drain and cool. Cut the tuna into chunks. Arrange the lettuce, beans, onion, tomatoes, eggs, tuna, and black olives in individual salad bowls. Arrange the anchovy fillets on the top. Mix together the dressing ingredients and spoon over the salad just before serving. Serve with crusty bread.

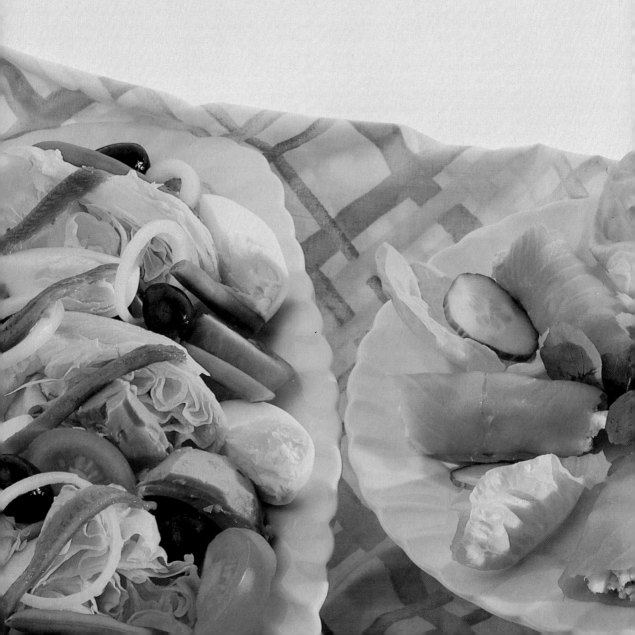

SMOKED SALMON AND EGG ROLLS
Serves 4

3 hard-boiled eggs
50 g/2 oz soft cheese, at room temperature
1 teaspoon whole grain mustard
salt and freshly ground black pepper
175 g/6 oz thinly sliced smoked salmon

garnish
lemon
lettuce

Chop the hard-boiled eggs and mix with the soft cheese, mustard, salt and pepper. Cut the salmon into 8 evenly sized pieces. Spread the egg mixture over the smoked salmon and roll up. Chill before serving. Serve with buttered rye bread, lemon and salad garnish.

LEEKS AND COURGETTES À LA GRECQUE
Serves 4

Be careful not to overcook the vegetables; they should be slightly crisp.

3 leeks, trimmed, washed and cut into
    7.5-cm/3-inch lengths
3 courgettes, thickly sliced
150 ml/¼ pint dry white wine
juice of 1 large lemon
sprig of thyme
1 bay leaf
½ teaspoon coriander seeds, crushed
½ teaspoon black peppercorns, crushed
½ teaspoon mustard seeds, crushed
5 tablespoons olive oil
salt and freshly ground black pepper
chopped fresh parsley to garnish

Cook the leeks and courgettes in boiling salted water for 3 minutes. Drain.

Heat the remaining ingredients in a saucepan with 150 ml/¼ pint water. Bring to the boil, cover and simmer for 5 minutes. Add the leeks and courgettes and cook for a further 10 minutes. Remove the leeks and courgettes using a slotted spoon and place in a serving dish. Boil the cooking liquor to reduce slightly, remove the bay leaf and thyme, pour the liquid over the leeks and courgettes and allow to cool. Serve chilled, sprinkled with parsley.

CHICKEN WALDORF SALAD
Serves 4

Try adding a little curry paste to the mayonnaise for extra flavour in this crunchy, crisp salad.

3 celery sticks
2 red skinned dessert apples
2 teaspoons lemon juice
3 tablespoons natural yogurt
3 tablespoons mayonnaise
salt and freshly ground black pepper
50 g/2 oz walnuts, chopped
225 g/8 oz cooked chicken, diced
1 small lettuce for garnish

Wash and slice the celery. Chop the apples, removing the core, and lightly toss in lemon juice. Mix together the yogurt, mayonnaise, salt and pepper. Add the celery, apples, walnuts and chicken and mix well. Serve on individual plates garnished with lettuce.

PEPPER FRITTATA
Serves 6

Frittata can be cooked in a square tin and cut into small squares to serve on cocktail sticks with drinks.

25 g/1 oz butter
1 red pepper, seeded and chopped
1 green pepper, seeded and chopped
½ bunch spring onions, chopped
1 clove garlic, crushed
6 eggs, beaten
4 cream crackers, crushed
3 tablespoons chopped fresh parsley
175 g/6 oz Cheddar cheese, grated
1 teaspoon salt
freshly ground black pepper
1 tomato, sliced

Grease a 20-cm/8-inch round cake tin and line the base with greased greaseproof paper. Heat the butter in a frying pan, add the peppers, spring onions and garlic and fry for about 5 minutes until soft but not browned. Transfer to a mixing bowl, cool slightly, then add remaining ingredients except the tomato. Pour into the prepared tin and arrange tomato slices on the top. Bake in a moderate oven (180°C, 350°F, gas 4) for 35-40 minutes until set. When the dish is cool, turn out and cut into wedges. Serve with salad garnish.

CAESAR SALAD
Serves 4 to 6

A really more-ish salad to get the taste buds going for the next course. Assemble at the last minute to prevent the croutons getting soggy. For a more substantial snack add an avocado and some tuna.

1 cos lettuce
4 thick slices white bread, crusts removed
6 tablespoons oil
1 clove garlic, crushed
1 egg
1 teaspoon Worcestershire sauce
2 tablespoons lemon juice
4 tablespoons olive oil
salt and freshly ground black pepper
2 tablespoons grated Parmesan cheese

Wash the lettuce and shake dry. Tear into pieces and place in a salad bowl. Cut the bread into 1-cm/½-inch cubes and fry in the oil until golden. Add the garlic and stir well. Drain on absorbent kitchen paper. Cook the egg for 1 minute in boiling water. Remove and break into a small bowl, scooping out the partly set egg white with a spoon. Add the Worcestershire sauce, lemon juice, olive oil, salt and pepper. Beat until thick. Just before serving, add the croutons to the salad bowl, pour over the dressing and toss. Sprinkle the Parmesan cheese on top.

HOT STARTERS

LEEK AND BACON SOUFFLÉ

Serves 4

If you can make white sauce, you can make a soufflé. But be warned, it won't wait around. Have everyone seated, ready and waiting—they won't be disappointed.

40 g/1½ oz butter
100 g/4 oz smoked rindless streaky bacon, finely chopped
225 g/8 oz leeks, washed and finely chopped
25 g/1 oz plain flour
150 ml/¼ pint milk
3 eggs, separated
2 teaspoons English mustard
50 g/2 oz mature Cheddar cheese, grated
salt and freshly ground black pepper
1 egg white

Grease a 900-ml/1½-pint soufflé dish. Melt 15 g/½ oz of the butter in a frying pan, add the bacon and leeks and cook gently for about 5 minutes. Melt the remaining butter in a saucepan, stir in the flour and cook for 1 minute. Remove from the heat and gradually add the milk, stirring well between each addition. Return to the heat and bring slowly to the boil, stirring until thickened. Cool slightly, then beat in the egg yolks one at a time. Add the mustard, bacon, leeks, cheese, salt and pepper. Whisk the egg whites until they are stiff and stand in peaks. Fold one tablespoon of whisked egg white into the sauce using a metal spoon, then fold in the remainder. Pour into the soufflé dish and bake in a preheated moderately hot oven (200°C, 400°F, gas 6) for 35-40 minutes until well risen and golden and set. Serve immediately.

DEEP FRIED MUSHROOMS WITH GARLIC SAUCE

Serves 4

To achieve a more subtle garlic flavour, use just the garlic herb soft cheese and omit the clove of garlic.

350 g/12 oz button or small flat mushrooms
4 tablespoons seasoned flour
1 egg, beaten
100 g/4 oz fresh bread crumbs
oil for deep frying

garlic sauce
100 g/4 oz garlic herb soft cheese
1 clove garlic, crushed
4 tablespoons natural yogurt
1 tablespoon chopped parsley

Wipe mushrooms with damp absorbent kitchen paper and trim the stalks. Roll the mushrooms in seasoned flour. Shake off any excess and dip in the beaten egg; then coat in the bread crumbs, pressing them on firmly

Mix the sauce ingredients together and beat until smooth. Chill until required.

Deep fry the mushrooms in hot oil at 180°C/350°F for 2-3 minutes until golden and crisp. Drain and serve immediately with the sauce.

SPINACH TIMBALES WITH WALNUT SAUCE
Serves 6

The smooth texture of the timbales goes well with the nutty sauce.

450 g/1 lb fresh spinach or 225 g/8 oz frozen spinach, thawed
2 eggs, size 3
250 ml/8 fl oz double cream
¼ teaspoon grated nutmeg
salt and freshly ground black pepper

walnut sauce
100 g/4 oz walnut pieces
1 clove garlic, crushed
150 ml/¼ pint vegetable or chicken stock (see page 4)
150 ml/¼ pint single cream
1 teaspoon cornflour
salt and freshly ground black pepper
walnut halves to garnish

Trim the stalks from the spinach, wash it, and cook until tender in a large saucepan without adding any extra water. Drain and squeeze out any excess water. Purée the spinach in a blender or food processor; add the eggs, cream, nutmeg, salt and pepper and blend until smooth. Pour into six greased ramekin dishes. Bake in a preheated moderate oven (160°C, 325°F, gas 3) for about 30 minutes, until firm to the touch.

To make the sauce, spread the walnuts on a baking tray and place in the oven with the timbales for 20 minutes. Rub the walnuts in a clean tea towel to remove most of the skins. Place them in a blender or food processor with the garlic, stock, cream and cornflour; blend until smooth. Heat in a saucepan, but do not boil. Season to taste. To serve, run a knife around the ramekins and turn out the timbales onto warm plates. Pour the walnut sauce around the timbales, place a walnut half on the top and serve.

SPAGHETTI CARBONARA
Serves 4 to 5

Although fresh Parmesan is expensive, its flavour is far superior to the ready-grated variety. Grate fresh Parmesan and store it in the freezer. It remains free-flow so the quantity required can be easily removed.

2 tablespoons oil
25 g/1 oz butter
2 cloves garlic, halved
175 g/6 oz rindless smoked bacon, chopped
275 g/10 oz spaghetti
2 eggs
50 g/2 oz freshly grated Parmesan cheese
150 ml/¼ pint single cream
freshly ground black pepper

Heat the oil and butter in a frying pan, add the garlic and cook until golden. Remove the garlic and discard. Add the bacon and cook until crisp. Cook the spaghetti in boiling salted water until just tender, about 10 minutes. Drain and return to the saucepan. Mix together the eggs, Parmesan, cream, black pepper and bacon. Pour onto the spaghetti. Using two spoons toss the spaghetti in the sauce. The heat of the spaghetti should just thicken the sauce. If it has cooled down, gently re-heat, but do not boil as the eggs will curdle. Serve in warmed shallow dishes with extra Parmesan and black pepper.

FUSILLI WITH SEAFOOD
Serves 4

Fusilli are pasta spirals. For variety, try other shapes such as conchiglie (shells), farfalle (bows) and penne (quills).

1 medium onion, chopped
2 tablespoons oil
1 clove garlic, crushed
450 g/1 lb tomatoes, peeled and chopped
½ teaspoon dried basil
salt and freshly ground black pepper
225 g/8 oz fusilli
100 g/4 oz frozen or canned mussels in natural
** juice, drained**
198-g/7-oz can shrimps in brine, drained
100-g/4 oz jar or can clams in natural juice,
** drained**
90-g/3½-oz can tuna, drained, roughly flaked
grated Parmesan cheese

Cook the onion in the oil until soft but not browned. Add the garlic and tomatoes and cook for about 15 minutes until soft and pulpy. Add the basil, salt and pepper. Cook the fusilli in boiling salted water until just tender, about 10 minutes. Drain. Add the mussels, shrimps, clams and tuna to the tomatoes and heat through. Divide the fusilli between 4 warmed shallow dishes and spoon the sauce on top. Serve with Parmesan cheese and black pepper.

MUSHROOM RISOTTO
Serves 6

For best results use Italian arborio or risotto rice which becomes sticky on the outside but stays firm in the centre, giving a creamy, moist risotto.

75 g/3 oz butter
1 small onion, chopped
350 g/12 oz Italian arborio or risotto rice
150 ml/¼ pint dry white wine
900 ml/1½ pints hot chicken stock (see page 4)
225 g/8 oz button mushrooms, wiped and sliced
grated Parmesan cheese
salt and freshly ground black pepper

Melt the butter in a large pan. Cook the onion until soft but not browned. Stir in the rice until well coated in butter. Turn the heat up and pour in the wine; cook until reduced by half. Pour in about 300 ml/½ pint chicken stock and cook, stirring until absorbed. Add another 300 ml/½ pint stock and cook, stirring until absorbed. Add the mushrooms with the remaining stock and cook until the rice has a slight bite to it. If the mixture becomes too dry, add more stock. Remove from the heat and add 3 tablespoons of Parmesan cheese, salt and plenty of dark pepper to taste. Serve immediately with extra Parmesan and ground black pepper.

COD AND SPINACH RAMEKINS
Serves 4

450 g/1 lb fresh spinach or 225 g/8 oz frozen
   spinach, thawed
salt and black pepper
¼ teaspoon grated nutmeg
50 g/2 oz butter
3 frozen cod steaks

cheese sauce
25 g/1 oz butter
25 g/1 oz flour
450 ml/¾ pint milk
100 g/4 oz Cheddar cheese, grated
salt and freshly ground black pepper

If using fresh spinach, trim the stalks from the
spinach, wash it, and cook until tender in a large
saucepan without adding any extra water. Drain well
and chop. If using frozen spinach, heat through and
squeeze out excess moisture. Season with salt, pepper
and nutmeg and stir in half the butter. Place in the
base of 4 large ramekin dishes. Fry the cod steaks in
the remaining butter for about 2 minutes each side,
cut into chunks and place on top of the spinach.

   To make the sauce, place the butter, flour and milk
in a saucepan. Bring to the boil slowly, beating with a
hand whisk continuously until sauce thickens. Remove from the heat and stir in half the cheese. Season
to taste. Pour the sauce over the fish and sprinkle with
remaining cheese. Cook in a preheated moderately
hot oven (190°C, 375°F, gas 5) for 20–25 minutes until
golden. Serve hot.

STUFFED AUBERGINES
Serves 4

The aubergines are blanched to take away the
bitterness they tend to have, also to cut down on
cooking time.

2 large aubergines
2 onions, chopped
2 tablespoons oil
1 clove garlic, crushed
25 g/1 oz pine nuts
100 g/4 oz ham, chopped
125 g/5 oz fresh white bread crumbs
2 tablespoons chopped fresh parsley
1 egg, beaten
salt and freshly ground black pepper
50 g/2 oz cheese, grated

Cut the aubergines in half, scoop out and reserve the
flesh leaving a 1-cm/½-inch shell. Blanch by cooking
in boiling salted water for 2 minutes. Drain. Stand
the shells in a greased shallow ovenproof dish.

   Cook the onion in the oil until soft but not
browned. Add the garlic, pine nuts and aubergine
flesh and cook for a further 4 minutes. Remove from
the heat and stir in the ham, bread crumbs, parsley,
egg, salt and pepper. Pile this mixture into the
aubergine shells and sprinkle with the cheese. Bake in
a preheated moderately hot oven (190°C, 375°F, gas
5) for about 40 minutes. Serve hot.

CHICKEN SATÉ
Serves 4

In Bali, where I first tasted saté, the chicken skewers are brought to the table on a small clay barbecue. Quite spectacular! To make coconut milk, dissolve 50 g/2 oz creamed coconut in 150 ml/¼ pint hot water.

3 boneless, skinless chicken breasts

marinade
1 clove garlic, crushed
2 tablespoons soy sauce
2 tablespoons water

peanut sauce
1 small onion, chopped
1 teaspoon chilli powder
100 g/4 oz crunchy peanut butter
1 tablespoon oil
175 ml/6 fl oz coconut milk
1 tablespoon lemon juice
1 tablespoon soy sauce
1 tablespoon brown sugar
salt

garnish
lime wedges
chilli, finely chopped

Cut the chicken into strips 7.5 cm/3 inch × 1 cm/½ inch and thread onto skewers concertina fashion. Arrange the skewers on a flat plate. Mix together the marinade ingredients, pour over the skewers and marinate for about 1 hour, turning occasionally.

To make the sauce, place the onion, chilli, peanut butter and oil in a liquidiser or food processor to make a paste. Transfer to a frying pan and heat the paste. Stir in the coconut milk and cook until the sauce is thick but not dry.

Grill the chicken skewers or cook on a barbecue for about 5 minutes each side. Stir the lemon juice, soy sauce and brown sugar into the peanut sauce. Heat through and add salt to taste. Serve the sauce poured over the skewers garnished with wedges of lime and finely chopped chilli.

MONK FISH AND SCALLOP KEBABS
Serves 4

Fish kebabs can be tricky as the fish tends to fall off; use a firm fish like monk fish.

4 large scallops
350 g/12 oz monk fish, skinned and boned
4 rashers rindless streaky bacon
1 lemon

marinade
2 tablespoons lemon juice
salt and pepper
2 tablespoons olive oil
125 ml/¼ pint white wine

Cut the scallops in half and cut the monk fish into cubes. Mix together the marinade ingredients, pour over the fish, cover and chill for 2 hours. Drain the fish and reserve the marinade for basting. Cut the bacon rashers in half and stretch them using the blade of a knife. Wrap each scallop half in bacon and thread onto 4 skewers with the monk fish and lemon cut into wedges. Grill for about 10 minutes, turning and basting with the marinade. Serve hot with tartare sauce.

SCAMPI IN TOMATO SAUCE
Serves 4

Prawns can be used instead of scampi, if liked.

1 small onion, chopped
1 celery stick
2 tablespoons olive oil
1 clove garlic, crushed
225-g/8-oz can tomatoes
1 tablespoon tomato purée
1 teaspoon sugar
pinch of dried oregano
salt and freshly ground black pepper
450 g/1 lb shelled cooked scampi

Cook the onion and celery in the oil until soft but not browned. Add the garlic, tomatoes and their juice, tomato purée, sugar, oregano, salt and pepper. Bring to the boil, cover and simmer for about 20 minutes. Purée in a liquidiser or food processor and return to a clean saucepan. Add the scampi and simmer for a further 5 minutes. Serve with a small portion of boiled rice.

MOULES MARINIÈRE
Serves 4

If mussels are overcooked, they become leathery, so cook over a high heat and time carefully. They should also be cooked on the day of purchase.

1.5 kg/3 lb fresh mussels
a handful of fine oatmeal or plain flour
6 tablespoons dry white wine
1 small onion, finely chopped
freshly ground black pepper
25 g/1 oz butter
1 tablespoon plain flour
chopped parsley

Soak the mussels in a bucket of water containing the oatmeal or flour for several hours. Tap any open shells sharply. If they fail to close, they are dead and should be discarded. Scrub the shells thoroughly and scrape off the 'beards' or protruding black threads. Wash the mussels in several changes of water to remove any grit.

Simmer the wine and onion together in a large saucepan to soften the onion. Add the mussels, cover and cook over a high heat for about 3 minutes, shaking the pan from time to time. Discard any mussels which remain closed. Transfer the mussels to warmed soup bowls or shallow dishes, reserving the cooking liquid.

Mix together the butter and flour to form a paste. Add this little by little to the cooking liquid, and return to the heat, stirring continuously, until thickened. Add pepper to taste and pour over the mussels. Sprinkle with parsley. Serve with lots of crusty bread to mop up the juices.

BROCCOLI AND TOMATO QUICHES
Serves 4

Cheese pastry is used in this recipe for extra flavour and crispness; however, the cheese can be omitted and plain or wholemeal shortcrust can be used instead.

cheese pastry
225 g/8 oz plain flour
pinch of salt
generous pinch of cayenne
100 g/4 oz butter or margarine
100 g/4 oz hard Cheddar cheese, finely grated
1 egg, size 3, beaten

filling
3 eggs, size 3
50 g/2 oz garlic herb soft cheese, at room temperature
150 ml/¼ pint milk
salt and freshly ground black pepper
150 g/6 oz broccoli, cooked
2 tomatoes, sliced

To make the pastry, sift together the flour, salt and cayenne. Rub in the fat until the mixture resembles fine bread crumbs. Add the cheese and beaten egg and mix to a firm dough. Turn onto a lightly floured surface and knead as little as possible until smooth. Roll out to 5-mm/¼-inch thickness and line four small quiche tins. Chill whilst preparing the filling.

Beat the eggs into the garlic herb cheese; then add the milk, salt and pepper. Cut the broccoli into 2-cm/1-inch pieces and divide between the quiche tins with the tomato slices. Pour the egg mixture over the top and cook in a preheated moderately hot oven (190°C, 375°F, gas 5) for about 20 minutes until golden and set. Serve warm.

STIR FRIED PRAWNS
Serves 4

A quick, colourful starter. Cook over a high heat, stirring all the time, to seal in the flavours and to retain colour and texture to the vegetables.

3 tablespoons sunflower oil
1 small yellow pepper, seeded and cut into
  strips
1 small green pepper, seeded and cut into strips
4 spring onions, cut diagonally
225 g/8 oz large peeled cooked prawns
2 tablespoons light soy sauce
1 tablespoon lemon juice
salt and freshly ground black pepper

garnish
fresh dill
unpeeled cooked prawns

Heat the oil in a wok or large frying pan. Add the
yellow and green peppers and cook over a high heat,
stirring, for 1 minute. Add the spring onions and
cook for a further minute. Add the prawns and cook
for a further minute. Mix together the soy sauce,
lemon juice, salt and pepper. Pour into the pan, stir
well and simmer to reduce the liquid by half. Spoon
onto warmed serving plates and serve immediately
with toast or crusty bread.

STUFFED MUSHROOMS
Serves 4

Flat mushrooms have much more flavour than
button mushrooms and the larger the mushroom the
easier it is to stuff.

12 medium or 8 large flat mushrooms
75 g/3 oz butter
1 large onion, finely chopped
1 clove garlic, crushed
75 g/3 oz rindless smoked bacon, finely
  chopped
75 g/ 3 oz fresh brown bread crumbs
5 tablespoons choppped parsley
75 g/3 oz Cheddar cheese, grated
4 tablespoons Parmesan cheese, grated
salt and freshly ground black pepper
parsley to garnish

Remove stalks from the mushrooms and chop. Wipe
the mushroom caps with damp absorbent kitchen
paper and place them on a baking tray. Melt the
butter in a pan. Add the onion, garlic, bacon and
mushroom stalks and cook gently until onion is soft.
Remove from the heat. Stir in the bread crumbs,
parsley and cheeses. Mix well and season to taste.
Spoon the mixture onto the mushroom caps. Bake in
a preheated moderately hot oven (200°C, 400°F, gas
6) for 10-15 minutes until the mushrooms are just
cooked. Serve hot garnished with parsley.

DEEP FRIED CAMEMBERT WITH GREEN FIGS

Serves 4

When you break open the crisp coating, soft Camembert oozes out. It's delicious and filling, so follow with a light main course. Cranberry sauce or a tart gooseberry sauce can be served instead of the figs.

450 g/1 lb Camembert cheese, well chilled
4 tablespoons seasoned flour
1 egg, beaten
100 g/4 oz fresh white bread crumbs
425-g/15-oz can green figs
oil for deep frying

Cut the Camembert into 8 wedges. Coat each piece in flour; then dip in beaten egg, followed by bread crumbs, pressing them on firmly.

Slice the green figs and arrange on four serving plates. Deep fry the Camembert four at a time in hot oil 180°C/350°F for about 3 minutes until golden and crisp. Drain and serve immediately with the figs.

FLAMENCO BAKED EGGS

Serves 4

The secret of getting a firm white and soft yolk is to heat the dishes in the oven before adding the eggs.

4 eggs
50 g/2 oz red pepper, seeded and chopped
50 g/2 oz green pepper, seeded and chopped
25 g/1 oz butter
1 tomato, peeled and chopped
salt and freshly ground pepper
150 ml/¼ pint double cream
50 g/2 oz cheese, grated

Butter 4 ramekin dishes and heat them in a moderate oven (180°C, 350°F, gas 4). Cook the peppers in the butter until soft but not browned. Stir in the tomato, salt and pepper. Place a spoonful of this mixture in the base of each ramekin. Crack an egg into each dish, and stand them in a roasting tin. Pour in sufficient boiling water to come halfway up the sides of the dishes. Bake for 6 minutes. Spoon cream over the top of each egg and sprinkle with cheese. Cook for a further 2 minutes. Serve immediately.

LEMON BUTTER MUSHROOMS
Serves 4

350 g/12 oz button mushrooms
50 g/2 oz butter
3 tablespoons lemon juice
½ teaspoon finely grated lemon rind
freshly ground black pepper
1 tablespoon chopped fresh parsley
lemon wedges to garnish

Wipe the mushrooms with damp absorbent kitchen paper and place in a saucepan with the butter, lemon juice, lemon rind and plenty of black pepper. Cover the pan, bring to the boil and simmer for 5 minutes. Serve warm sprinkled with parsley. Garnish with lemon wedges and serve with hot herb bread (see page 9).

BARBECUED SPARE RIBS
Serves 4

Have dishes of warm water with slices of lemon floating in them and plenty of paper napkins on hand to rinse sticky fingers.

1 tablespoon redcurrant jelly
1 tablespoon soy sauce
2 tablespoons Worcestershire sauce
1 teaspoon mustard powder
1 tablespoon honey
½ teaspoon Tabasco sauce
2 tablespoons vinegar
1 clove garlic, crushed
1 tablespoon tomato ketchup
salt and freshly ground black pepper
1 kg/2 lb pork spare ribs

garnish
1 small crisp lettuce, shredded
1 large carrot, grated

Melt the redcurrant jelly in a saucepan over a low heat. Remove from the heat and stir in remaining ingredients except the ribs. Place the ribs in a roasting tin or ovenproof dish and pour over the marinade. Leave for at least 4 hours, turning occasionally. Cook in a preheated moderate oven (160°C, 325°F, gas 3) for about 40 minutes, basting occasionally. Increase the heat to moderately hot (200°C, 400°F, gas 6) for about 15 minutes until the ribs are crisp on the outside. Serve hot on a bed of shredded lettuce and grated carrot.

SWEET AND SOUR CHICKEN PANCAKES

Serves 8

pancakes
100 g/4 oz plain flour
pinch of salt
1 egg
300 ml/½ pint milk
lard or oil for frying

filling
1 small onion, chopped
1 tablespoon oil
75 g/3 oz mushrooms, sliced
75 g/3 oz bean sprouts
75 g/3 oz cooked chicken, chopped
75 g/3 oz canned pineapple pieces
2 tablespoons pineapple juice
2 teaspoons soy sauce
salt and freshly ground black pepper

To make the pancakes, sift the flour and salt into a bowl. Make a well in the centre, add the egg, and a little of the milk and beat with a wooden spoon, gradually incorporating the flour. As the mixture thickens, gradually add the remaining milk. Beat well. Heat a little lard or oil in a small frying pan.

When the oil is hot, pour in enough batter to cover the base of the pan thinly. Cook over a high heat for about 1 minute until browned underneath. Toss or turn the pancake over and cook the other side about ½ minute. Repeat to make 8 pancakes.

To make the filling, cook the onion in the oil until soft. Turn up the heat and add the mushrooms, bean sprouts, chicken and pineapple and cook, stirring, for about 3 minutes. Add the pineapple juice, soy sauce, salt and pepper and cook for a further minute. Divide the filling between the pancakes and roll or fold up. Place in a greased ovenproof dish and heat in a preheated moderately hot oven (190°C, 375°F, gas 5) for about 10 minutes.

DEVILLED CHICKEN LIVERS

Serves 4

The easiest way to chop chicken livers is to cut them with kitchen scissors.

450 g/1 lb chicken livers
50 g/2 oz butter
2 teaspoons Dijon mustard
salt and freshly ground black pepper
2 teaspoons Worcestershire sauce
½ teaspoon vinegar
chopped parsley to garnish

Trim the chicken livers, rinse and dry on absorbent kitchen paper. Chop the chicken livers and cook gently in the butter for about 5 minutes, stirring frequently, until firm but still pink inside. Add the mustard, salt and pepper, Worcestershire sauce and vinegar. Stir well and cook for a further 2 minutes. Serve on hot buttered toast, sprinkled with parsley.

SPICY LAMB TRIANGLES
Serves 6

Phyllo, or streudel pastry, can be bought from delicatessens and Greek and Turkish shops. It dries out quickly, so when not using, keep well covered.

filling
225 g/8 oz minced lamb
½ clove garlic, crushed
½ teaspoon turmeric
½ teaspoon ground cumin
pinch of cayenne
½ teaspoon salt
freshly ground black pepper
1 tablespoon mango chutney

pastry
5 sheets of phyllo pastry
50 g/2 oz butter, melted

garnish
radishes
parsley

Fry the mince in a non-stick frying pan without adding any extra fat. Drain off any fat. Stir in the garlic, turmeric, cumin, cayenne, salt and pepper and cook for a further 2 minutes. Remove from the heat and stir in the chutney. Cool.

Lay a sheet of phyllo pastry on a clean work surface and brush with melted butter. Keep the other sheets of pastry covered to prevent them from drying out. Using a sharp knife, cut the pastry lengthways into four equal strips. Place a teaspoonful of the meat mixture in the lefthand corner of each strip. Fold the corner of pastry over the filling to form a triangle, continue folding over the pastry strip to form a triangular package. Place on a greased baking tray. Repeat with the remaining sheets of dough. Bake in a preheated moderately hot oven (200°C, 400°F, gas 6) for about 20 minutes until golden and crisp. Serve hot with natural yogurt, garnished with radishes and parsley.

GINGERED CHICKEN WINGS
Serves 4

Chicken wings are not only economical, but the meat on them is very sweet and tender.

12 chicken wings
2 tablespoons oil
3 spring onions, finely chopped
4 tablespoons light soy sauce
4 tablespoons dry sherry
2 tablespoons tomato ketchup
25 g/1 oz fresh ginger, grated
salt and freshly ground black pepper

Prick the skins of the chicken wings with a fork. Mix together remaining ingredients and pour over chicken in a large roasting tin or ovenproof dish. Leave to marinate for about 3 hours. Cook in a preheated moderate oven (180°C, 350°F, gas 4) for 35–40 minutes, turning occasionally, until chicken is cooked and skin is golden. Serve hot.

GOAT'S CHEESE PUFFS
Serves 4

These are great if you don't want to serve a formal starter, but want something tasty to nibble with drinks. Try filling them with taramasalata or chopped tomato and black olive.

50 g/2 oz butter
150 ml/¼ pint milk and water mixed
65 g/2½ oz plain flour
generous pinch of salt
2 eggs, beaten
75 g/3 oz goat's cheese, cut into small chunks
paprika to garnish

Gently heat the butter, milk and water until the butter has melted. Turn up the heat, bring to the boil and tip in the flour and salt. Remove from the heat and beat vigorously until the mixture leaves the sides of the pan. Cool slightly. Beat in the egg a little at a time until smooth and glossy. Beat in the cheese. Place teaspoonfuls of mixture on greased baking trays and bake in a preheated moderately hot oven (200°C, 400°F, gas 6) for 10–12 minutes until well risen and golden. Make a slit in the side of each puff with a sharp knife. Return to the heat of the turned out oven for a further 10 minutes. Serve warm sprinkled with paprika.

PRAWN PARCELS
Serves 6

This showy starter has a crisp coating filled with a delicious prawn sauce. They freeze well uncooked and can be fried from frozen.

pastry
200 ml/7 fl oz water
25 g/1 oz butter
150 g/5 oz plain flour
½ teaspoon salt

filling
25 g/1 oz butter
25 g/1 oz flour
200 ml/7 fl oz milk
100 g/4 oz prawns, chopped
salt and freshly ground black pepper
1 tablespoon lemon juice
1 tablespoon chopped parsley

coating
1 egg, beaten
100 g/4 oz fresh white bread crumbs
oil for deep frying

To make the pastry, bring the water and butter to the boil. When the butter has melted, add the flour and salt and mix well. Remove from the heat and beat until mixture leaves the sides of the pan. Turn out of the pan, cover in cling film and allow to cool.

To make the filling, place the butter, flour and milk in a saucepan. Bring to the boil slowly, beating with a hand whisk continuously until sauce thickens. Remove from the heat and stir in prawns, salt and pepper, lemon juice and parsley. Cover and cool.

Roll out the pastry thinly on a lightly floured surface and cut into twelve 10-cm/4-inch rounds. Place a little filling in the centre of each round. Brush the edge of the pastry with water and fold in half. Press to seal. Dip in the beaten egg and coat with bread crumbs. Chill for 30 minutes. Heat the oil to 180°C/360°F and fry the prawn parcels for 3 minutes until golden. Drain and serve.

INDEX